COUNTRIES OF THE WORLD

Scotland

by Bryan Langdo

BELLWETHER MEDIA • MINNEAPOLIS, MN

Blastoff! Readers are carefully developed by literacy experts to build reading stamina and move students toward fluency by combining standards-based content with developmentally appropriate text.

 **Level 1** provides the most support through repetition of high-frequency words, light text, predictable sentence patterns, and strong visual support.

 **Level 2** offers early readers a bit more challenge through varied sentences, increased text load, and text-supportive special features.

 **Level 3** advances early-fluent readers toward fluency through increased text load, less reliance on photos, advancing concepts, longer sentences, and more complex special features.

★ **Blastoff! Universe**

Reading Level

Grade K → Grades 1–3 → Grade 4

This edition first published in 2025 by Bellwether Media, Inc.

No part of this publication may be reproduced in whole or in part without written permission of the publisher. For information regarding permission, write to Bellwether Media, Inc., Attention: Permissions Department, 6012 Blue Circle Drive, Minnetonka, MN 55343.

Library of Congress Cataloging-in-Publication Data

LC record for Scotland available at: https://lccn.loc.gov/2024012095

Text copyright © 2025 by Bellwether Media, Inc. BLASTOFF! READERS and associated logos are trademarks and/or registered trademarks of Bellwether Media, Inc. Bellwether Media is a division of Chrysalis Education Group.

Editor: Suzane Nguyen   Designer: Laura Sowers

Printed in the United States of America, North Mankato, MN.

Table of Contents

All About Scotland	4
Land and Animals	6
Life in Scotland	12
Scotland Facts	20
Glossary	22
To Learn More	23
Index	24

All About Scotland

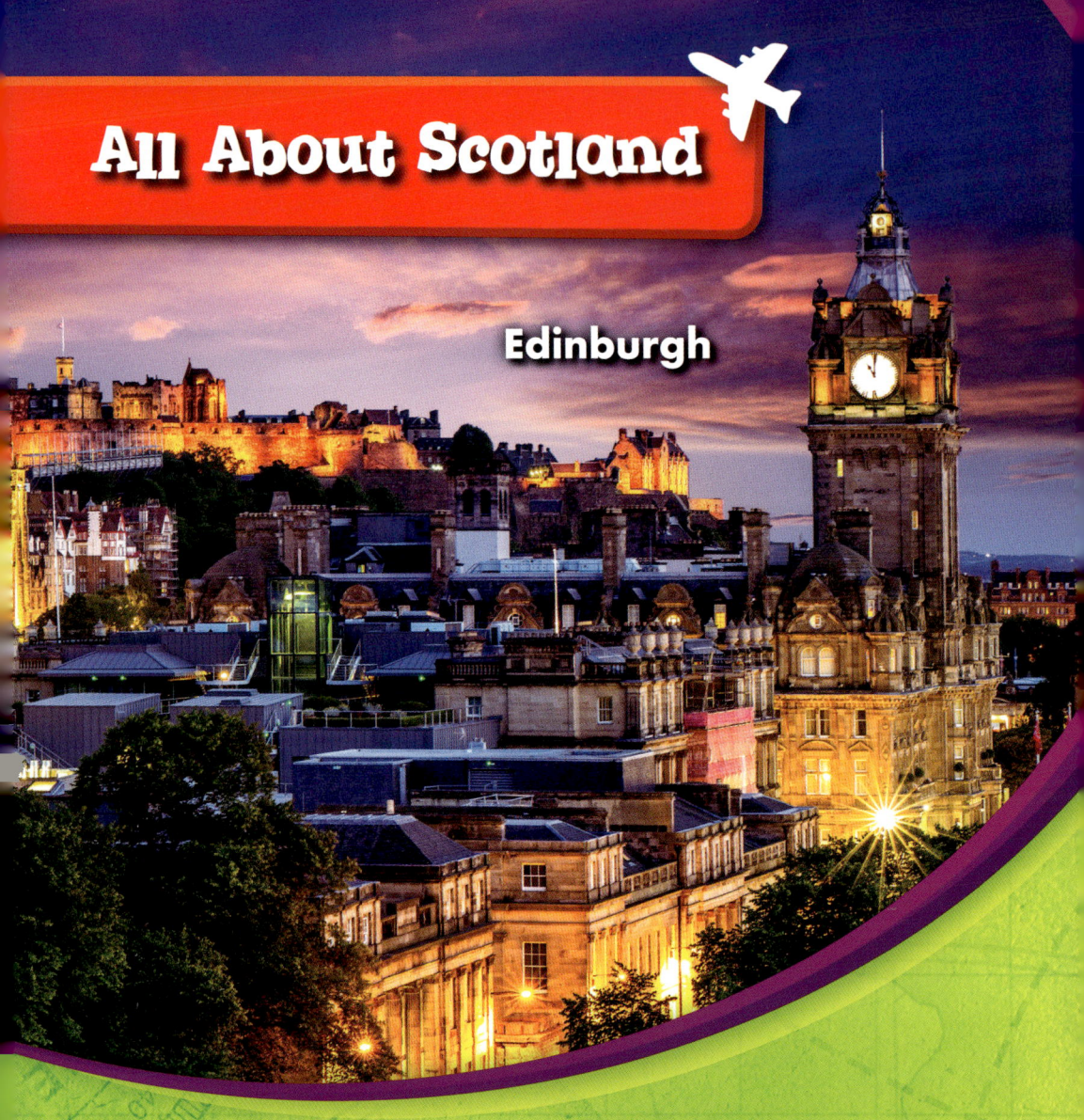

Edinburgh

Scotland is in Europe. It is part of the **United Kingdom**. Edinburgh is Scotland's capital city.

Scotland is known for bagpipe music!

Land and Animals

Much of Scotland is **moorland**. The coast has many islands. There are also **fjords**.

The Highlands are in the north. The area has many mountains and lakes.

moorland

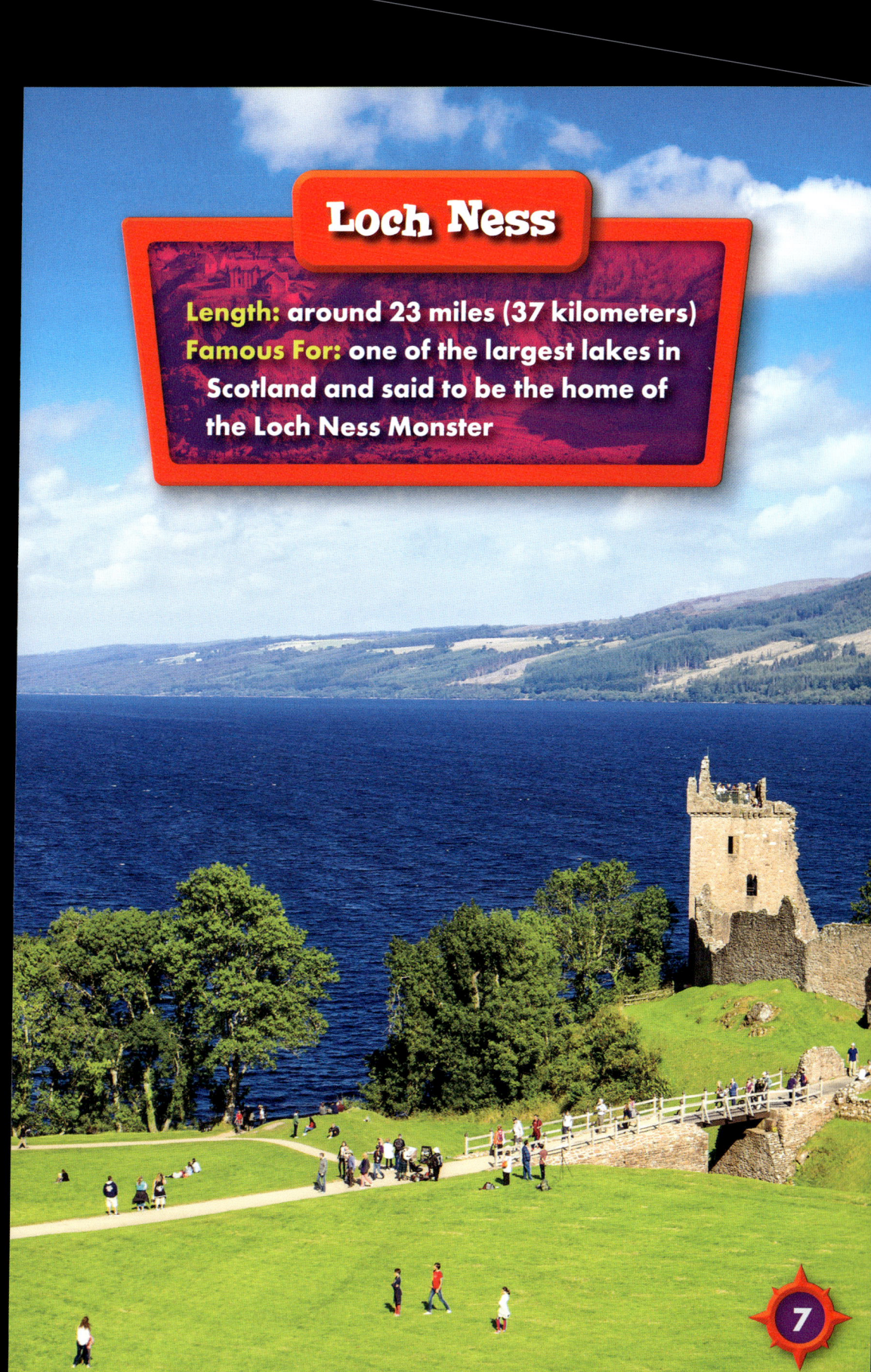

Loch Ness

Length: around 23 miles (37 kilometers)
Famous For: one of the largest lakes in Scotland and said to be the home of the Loch Ness Monster

Scotland is a **temperate** country. It gets a lot of rain.

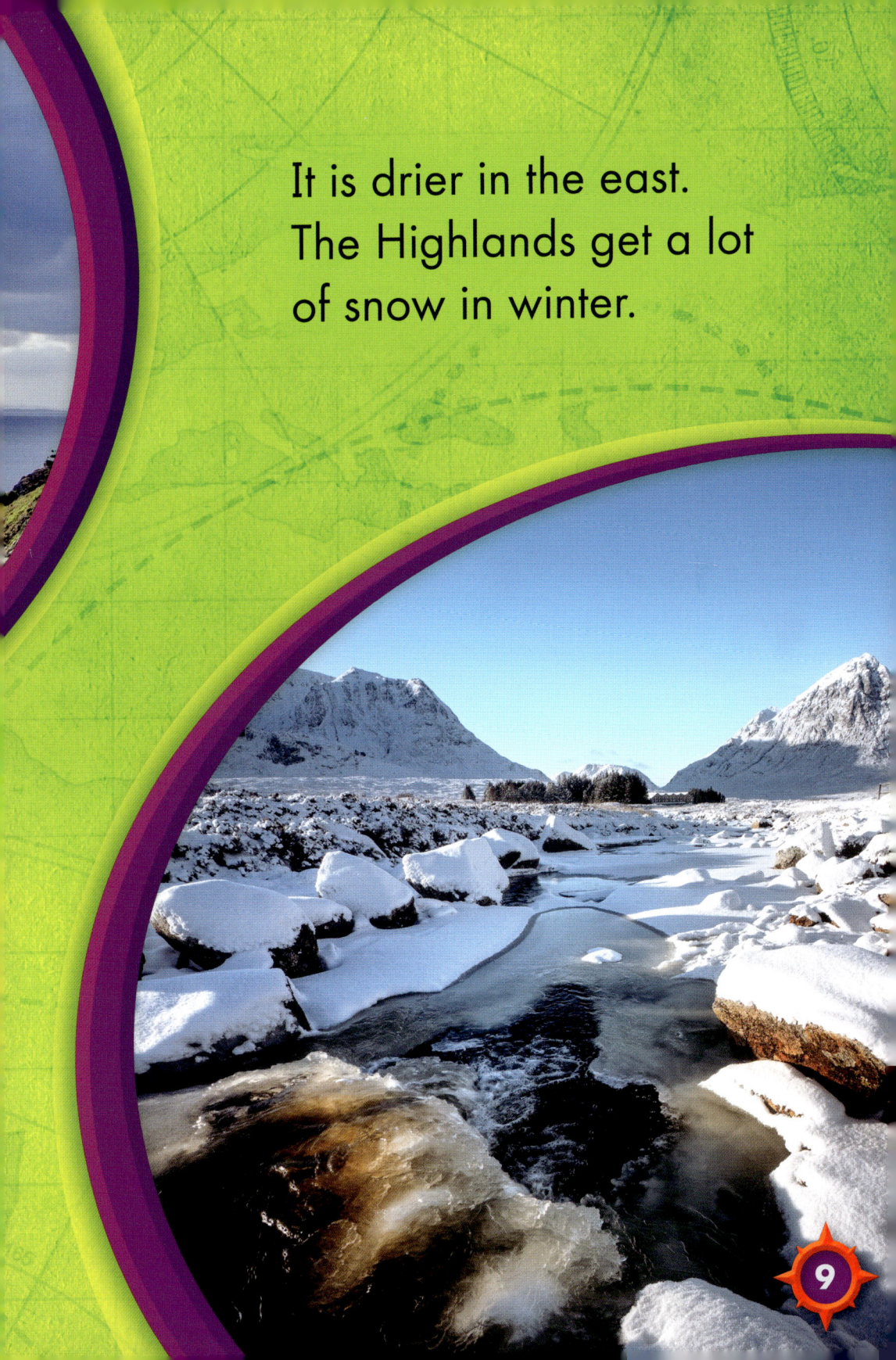

It is drier in the east. The Highlands get a lot of snow in winter.

Scotland has a lot of wildlife. Deer roam the Highlands.

Atlantic puffin

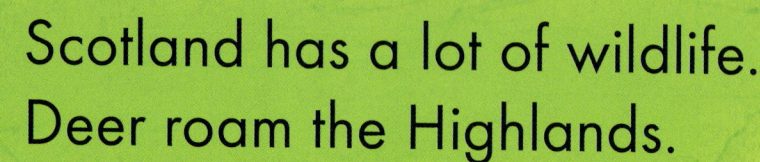

Hares and toads live near lakes. Puffins nest on cliffs.

Life in Scotland

Scots come from several **backgrounds**. Most speak English. Some speak Scottish Gaelic.

Most Scots live in cities. The biggest city is Glasgow.

Glasgow

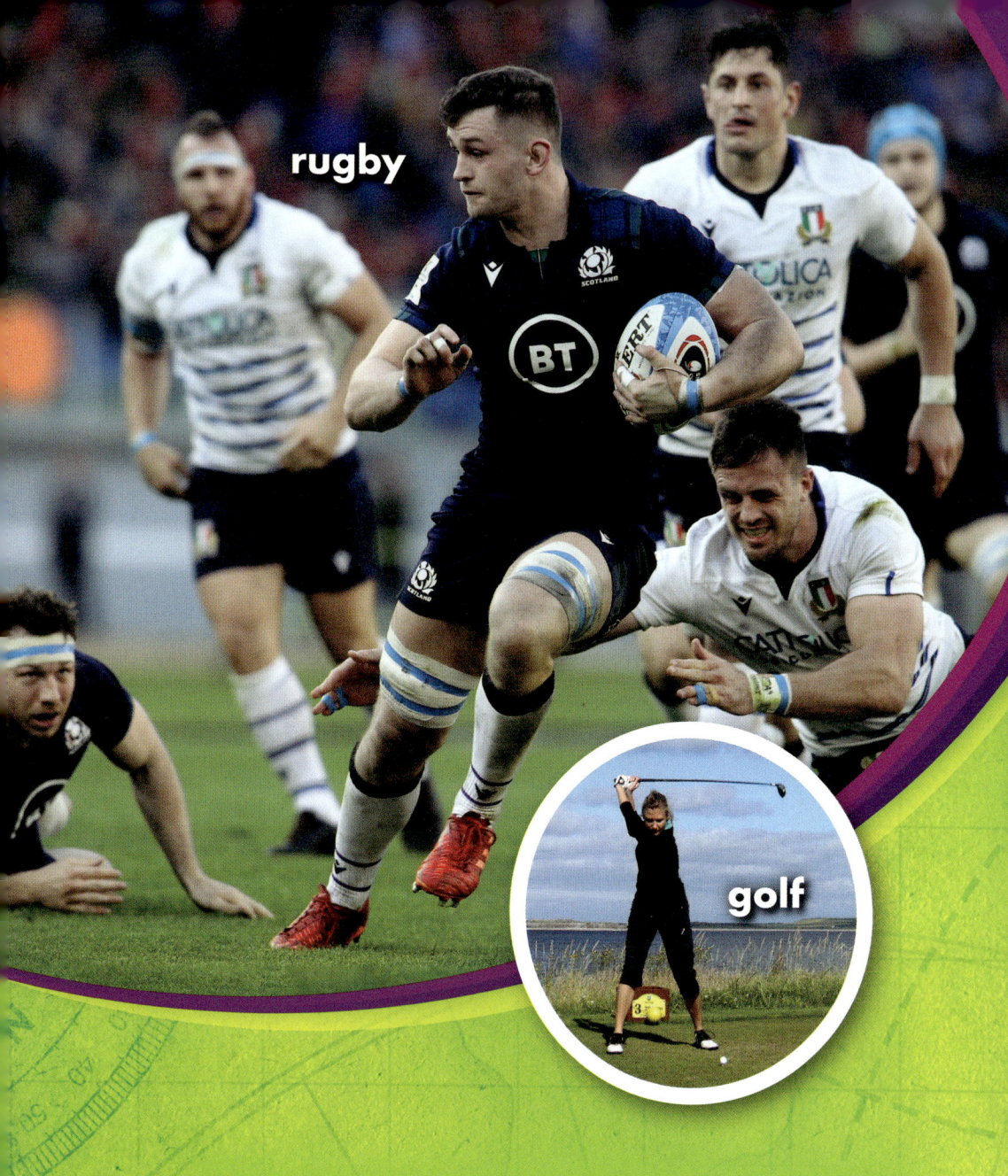

rugby

golf

Sports are popular in Scotland. Scots like soccer, rugby, and golf.

Scotland is home to many writers and poets. Scots enjoy **traditional** music at **festivals**.

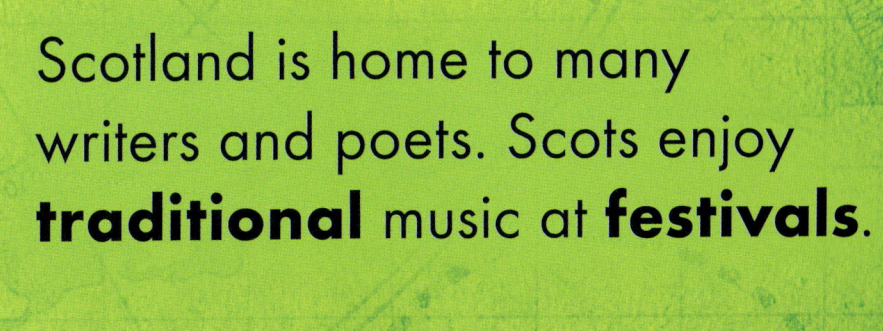

Scotland has many tasty foods. Haggis is meat with spices. Scottish porridge is oats.

Scottish Foods

haggis

Scottish porridge

Cullen skink

cranachan

haggis

Cullen skink is a fish soup. *Cranachan* is a dessert with raspberries.

The Highland Games happen in summer. Some people race. Others do the hammer toss.

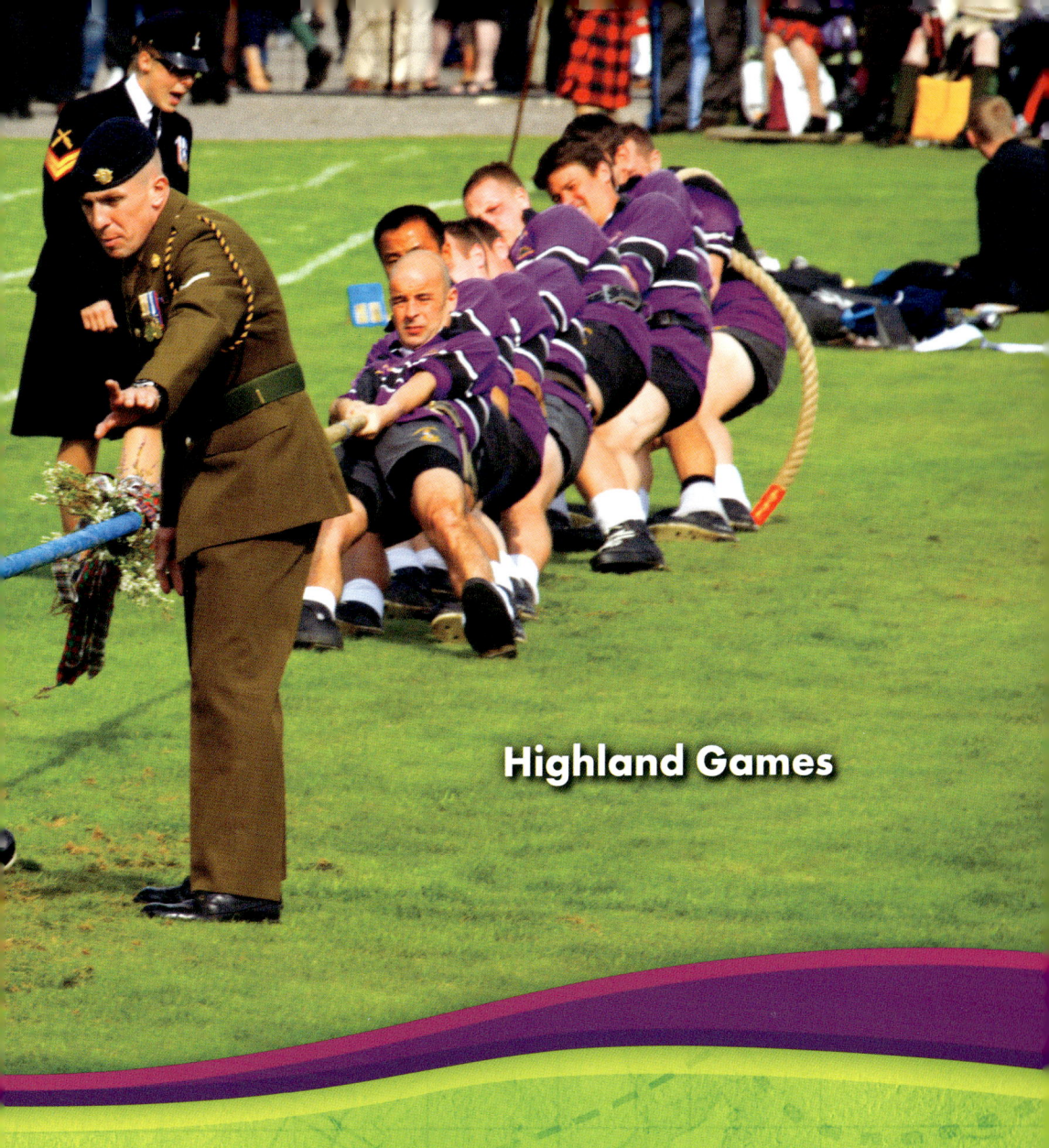

Highland Games

November 30 is St. Andrew's Day. People enjoy a big dinner. Scots love their **heritage**!

Scotland Facts

Size:
30,087 square miles
(77,925 square kilometers)

Population:
5,436,600 (2022)

National Holiday:
St. Andrew's Day (November 30)

Main Languages:
English, Scottish Gaelic

Capital City:
Edinburgh

Famous Face

Name: Ewan McGregor

Famous For: an award-winning actor who played Obi-Wan Kenobi in the Star Wars movies

Religions

- other 18%
- Muslim 2%
- none 48%
- Roman Catholic 12%
- Church of Scotland 20%

Top Landmarks

Calanais Standing Stones

Edinburgh Castle

Glenfinnan Viaduct

Glossary

backgrounds—people's experiences, knowledge and family histories

festivals—times of celebration

fjords—narrow inlets from the sea between cliffs or steep slopes

heritage—the backgrounds and beliefs that are part of the history of a group of people

moorland—open, wet land that is not good for farming

temperate—related to a mild climate that does not have extreme heat or cold

traditional—related to customs, ideas, or beliefs handed down from one generation to the next

United Kingdom—a country in Europe that includes England, Scotland, Wales, and Northern Ireland

To Learn More

AT THE LIBRARY

An Amazing Animal Atlas of Scotland. Edinburgh, Scotland: Kelpies, 2020.

Hansen, Grace. *Edinburgh Castle.* Minneapolis, Minn.: Abdo Kids, 2022.

MacPhail, David. *An Amazing Illustrated Atlas of Scotland.* Edinburgh, Scotland: Kelpies, 2022.

ON THE WEB

FACTSURFER

Factsurfer.com gives you a safe, fun way to find more information.

1. Go to www.factsurfer.com.
2. Enter "Scotland" into the search box and click 🔍.
3. Select your book cover to see a list of related content.

Index

animals, 10, 11
capital (see Edinburgh)
cities, 4, 12
coast, 6
Edinburgh, 4, 5
English, 12
Europe, 4
festivals, 15
fjords, 6
food, 16, 17
Glasgow, 12
golf, 14
Highland Games, 18, 19
Highlands, 6, 9, 10
islands, 6
lakes, 6, 7, 11
Loch Ness, 7
map, 5
moorland, 6
mountains, 6
music, 5, 15
people, 12, 14, 15, 18, 19
poets, 15
rain, 8
rugby, 14
say hello, 13
Scotland facts, 20–21
Scottish Gaelic, 12, 13
snow, 9
soccer, 14
St. Andrew's Day, 19
United Kingdom, 4
winter, 9
writers, 15

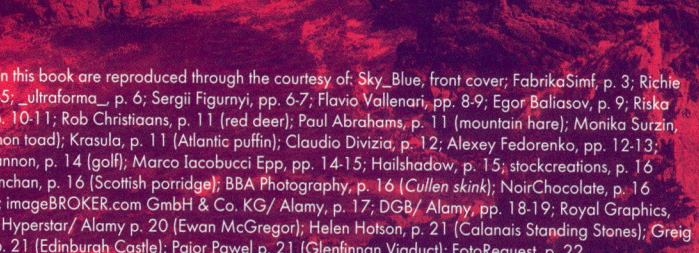

The images in this book are reproduced through the courtesy of: Sky_Blue, front cover; FabrikaSimf, p. 3; Richie Chan, pp. 4-5; _ultraforma_, p. 6; Sergii Figurnyi, pp. 6-7; Flavio Vallenari, pp. 8-9; Egor Baliasov, p. 9; Riska Parakeet, pp. 10-11; Rob Christiaans, p. 11 (red deer); Paul Abrahams, p. 11 (mountain hare); Monika Surzin, p. 11 (common toad); Krasula, p. 11 (Atlantic puffin); Claudio Divizia, p. 12; Alexey Fedorenko, pp. 12-13; Graeme Shannon, p. 14 (golf); Marco Iacobucci Epp, pp. 14-15; Hailshadow, p. 15; stockcreations, p. 16 (haggis); bonchan, p. 16 (Scottish porridge); BBA Photography, p. 16 (*Cullen skink*); NoirChocolate, p. 16 (*cranachan*); imageBROKER.com GmbH & Co. KG/ Alamy, p. 17; DGB/ Alamy, pp. 18-19; Royal Graphics, p. 20 (flag); Hyperstar/ Alamy p. 20 (Ewan McGregor); Helen Hotson, p. 21 (Calanais Standing Stones); Greig Gallagher, p. 21 (Edinburgh Castle); Pajor Pawel p. 21 (Glenfinnan Viaduct); FotoRequest, p. 22.